The Calendar

A Week

by Patricia J. Murphy

Consulting Editor: Gail Saunders-Smith, PhD

Capstone
press
Mankato, Minnesota

Pebble Books are published by Capstone Press,
151 Good Counsel Drive, P.O. Box 669, Mankato, Minnesota 56002.
www.capstonepress.com

1 2 3 4 5 6 10 09 08 07 06 05

Library of Congress Cataloging-in-Publication Data
Murphy, Patricia J., 1963–
    A week / by Patricia J. Murphy.
    p. cm.—(The calendar)
    Includes bibliographical references and index.
    ISBN 0-7368-3627-6 (hardcover)
    1. Week—Juvenile literature. I. Title.
CE13.M87 2005
529'.2—dc22   2004011901

Note to Parents and Teachers

The Calendar set supports national social studies and history standards related to time, place, and change. This book describes and illustrates a week. The images support early readers in understanding the text. The repetition of words and phrases helps early readers learn new words. This book also introduces early readers to subject-specific vocabulary words, which are defined in the Glossary section. Early readers may need assistance to read some words and to use the Table of Contents, Glossary, Read More, Internet Sites, and Index sections of the book.

Table of Contents

What Is a Week? 5
Weekdays 9
The Weekend 19

Glossary 22
Read More 23
Internet Sites 23
Index 24

THIS WEEK

Sunday	Don's Birthday
Monday	Field Trip
Tuesday	Sharing Time
Wednesday	Math Test
Thursday	Molly's Birthday
Friday	Spelling Test
Saturday	Jimmy's Birthday

What Is a Week?

A week lasts seven days.
Monday, Tuesday,
Wednesday, Thursday,
and Friday are weekdays.
Saturday and Sunday
make up the weekend.

The Calendar

January

Sunday	Monday	Tuesday	Wednesday	Thursday	Friday	Saturday
		1	2	3	4	5
6	7	8	9	10	11	12
13	14	15	16	17	18	19
20	21	22	23	24	25	26
27	28	29	30	31		

February

Sunday	Monday	Tuesday	Wednesday	Thursday	Friday	Saturday
					1	2
3	4	5	6	7	8	9
10	11	12	13	14	15	16
17	18	19	20	21	22	23
24	25	26	27	28		

March

Sunday	Monday	Tuesday	Wednesday	Thursday	Friday	Saturday
					1	2
3	4	5	6	7	8	9
10	11	12	13	14	15	16
17	18	19	20	21	22	23
24/31	25	26	27	28	29	30

April

Sunday	Monday	Tuesday	Wednesday	Thursday	Friday	Saturday
	1	2	3	4	5	6
7	8	9	10	11	12	13
14	15	16	17	18	19	20
21	22	23	24	25	26	27
28	29	30				

May

Sunday	Monday	Tuesday	Wednesday	Thursday	Friday	Saturday
			1	2	3	4
5	6	7	8	9	10	11
12	13	14	15	16	17	18
19	20	21	22	23	24	25
26	27	28	29	30	31	

June

Sunday	Monday	Tuesday	Wednesday	Thursday	Friday	Saturday
						1
2	3	4	5	6	7	8
9	10	11	12	13	14	15
16	17	18	19	20	21	22
23/30	24	25	26	27	28	29

July

Sunday	Monday	Tuesday	Wednesday	Thursday	Friday	Saturday
	1	2	3	4	5	6
7	8	9	10	11	12	13
14	15	16	17	18	19	20
21	22	23	24	25	26	27
28	29	30	31			

August

Sunday	Monday	Tuesday	Wednesday	Thursday	Friday	Saturday
				1	2	3
4	5	6	7	8	9	10
11	12	13	14	15	16	17
18	19	20	21	22	23	24
25	26	27	28	29	30	31

September

Sunday	Monday	Tuesday	Wednesday	Thursday	Friday	Saturday
1	2	3	4	5	6	7
8	9	10	11	12	13	14
15	16	17	18	19	20	21
22	23	24	25	26	27	28
29	30					

October

Sunday	Monday	Tuesday	Wednesday	Thursday	Friday	Saturday
		1	2	3	4	5
6	7	8	9	10	11	12
13	14	15	16	17	18	19
20	21	22	23	24	25	26
27	28	29	30	31		

November

Sunday	Monday	Tuesday	Wednesday	Thursday	Friday	Saturday
					1	2
3	4	5	6	7	8	9
10	11	12	13	14	15	16
17	18	19	20	21	22	23
24	25	26	27	28	29	30

December

Sunday	Monday	Tuesday	Wednesday	Thursday	Friday	Saturday
1	2	3	4	5	6	7
8	9	10	11	12	13	14
15	16	17	18	19	20	21
22	23	24	25	26	27	28
29	30	31				

The calendar shows that
about four weeks
make one month.
There are 52 weeks
in each year.

There is a little <u>beach</u> at the lake. We go there every <u>week</u>. I play with the other <u>children</u>. We like <u>feeding</u> the ducks. One day I had on my new <u>skirt</u>. It is as red as a <u>rose</u>. It is very <u>pretty</u>. That was the day a duck <u>slept</u> on my shoes! I wrote my friend a <u>letter</u> about that.

Weekdays

Don goes to school
on the weekdays.
On Monday, he learns
new spelling words.

On Tuesday afternoon,
Don helps his mom
wash the car.

On Wednesday morning,
Don feels sick.
He stays home
from school.

On Thursday evening,
Don and his friends
play games.

16

On Friday, Don takes
a spelling test.

The Weekend

The weekend starts
on Saturday.
Don and his mom
shop for groceries.

On Sunday, Don
and his family
eat lunch together.
Don goes back
to school tomorrow.

Glossary

afternoon—the time of day between noon and evening

calendar—a chart that shows all of the days, weeks, and months in a year; some calendars show one day, one week, or one month at a time.

day—a period of time that equals 24 hours; there are seven days in each week.

evening—the time of day between the late afternoon and the early part of the night

month—one of the 12 parts that make up a year; each month is from 28 to 31 days long.

morning—the time of day between midnight and noon

year—a period of 12 months; the year begins on January 1 and ends on December 31.

Read More

Kummer, Patricia K. *The Calendar.* Inventions that Shaped the World. New York: Franklin Watts, 2005.

Nelson, Robin. *A Week.* First Step Nonfiction. Minneapolis: Lerner, 2002.

Williams, Brian. *Calendars.* About Time. North Mankato, Minn.: Smart Apple Media, 2003.

Internet Sites

FactHound offers a safe, fun way to find Internet sites related to this book. All of the sites on FactHound have been researched by our staff.

Here's how:

1. Visit *www.facthound.com*

2. Type in this special code **0736836276** for age-appropriate sites. Or enter a search word related to this book for a more general search.

3. Click on the **Fetch It** button.

FactHound will fetch the best sites for you!

Index

afternoon, 11
calendar, 7
evening, 15
Friday, 5, 17
Monday, 5, 9
month, 7
morning, 13
Saturday, 5, 19

Sunday, 5, 21
Thursday, 5, 15
Tuesday, 5, 11
Wednesday, 5, 13
weekdays, 5, 9, 11, 13, 15, 17
weekend, 5, 19, 21
year, 7

Word Count: 115
Grade: 1
Early-Intervention Level: 9

Editorial Credits
Sarah L. Schuette, editor; Jennifer Bergstrom, set designer

Photo Credits
All photographs by James Photography/James Menk